# Life As It Happens

### Feel Alive

## Dr. Shweta Arora

BookLeaf Publishing

India | USA | UK

Made with ♥ on the BookLeaf Publishing Platform

www.bookleafpub.in

www.bookleafpub.com

# Dedication

This ensemble of little poems as they are called is more of an epiphany of all the experiences that I have been through ...whether great or some even not so great... these are the words that echoed in my heart and I have tried to compile them on paper.
This little collection of poems is therefore dedicated to LIFE as it Happened to me...and I hope the ones who read them get a touch of life as well and feel alive even if for a moment.. in it's real and true sense.

# Preface

This one is a humble and heartfelt attempt of mine.. a complete non writer, one who has always been a physician , a doctor, an ardent student, a learner. Despite having achieved so many things academically and professionally, there always felt a void inside me.. something inside me always craved to expressed myself through my words and feelings .And this little collection of poems felt like just the right thing to help me do so. Readers might find all of these poems naive and rightly so as I am nothing like any of the accomplished poets or writers.

This is just something from my heart to your heart...

# Acknowledgements

I would like to express my deepest gratitude to everyone who made this book possible.

Grateful to Book Leaf Publishers to have come up with such a wonderful idea of inspiring non writers like me and given a platform to put our thoughts on paper and showcase it to the world.

To my family whose unwavering support kept me going through the writing process despite my busy schedule as a doctor to look after my patients as my priority.

This book would not have been possible without the inspiration and selfless support and feedbacks from my Life partner  who has been patient enough to read my poems every single day of the process and stood by me throughout.

Last but not the least, thank you to my readers---- this book is for you!

# 1. True happiness-Childhood

Those were the days
Worry free and Carefree
Every day every moment full of life
Innocence at its peak
Love most selfless
Eyes beaming with glare of chuckles
Cheeks blushing with touch of Sun
Those refreshing mornings
Those sunny afternoons
Playful evenings
And peaceful night sleep
That was life in its most pure form
The way God wants us to live and feel life
How I wish we could once again go back to that phase
and take life in it's stride
Live Life as it Happens....

# 2. Growing up- Life Blooms

We grew as life grew
We learned, we grasped things
Everyday watched and learnt new things
With enthusiasm and curiosity
Curiosity of a child... just being curious in it's true sense
Made new friends, that bond stayed with us forever
Learnt the real meaning of friendship
We were yet to know hardship
Received some and imparted some Unconditional love
World opened up , we always showed up
Life felt like beaming with infinite possibilities
We were yet to learn it's nitty gritties
Life gave us everything
We weren't short of anything
Parents and family were all there.. we felt so secure
Life ..... Oh my darling... so pure!!!

# 3. Realms of Life

Picturesque as life is and can be
Grotesque as we can take it to be
It's filled with so many colours
Varied Shades of all the colours
Magnificent as a rainbow
So many and varied hues to show
Howsoever enthralled we may find it to be
The beauty of life lies in it to be
Essence of life is in flowing with it
Facing the heat and glowing with it
Living it and in it's realm
Just be yourself and hand it over your helm...

# 4. Sweet Bitter Life

As sweet as nectar
As bitter as gall
Whatever it tastes
However it feels
As certain as its existence
As sure as it's presence
This fruit of life
When you slowly cut it with a knife
You might find a new taste in it's every bite
One thing that it assures is a lot of delight
Cherish it's every flavour
Embrace it's every single endeavour
That's the only way you live it ,love it
If you have any doubt , shove it
Discover it's true meaning
And that's how life becomes healing...

# 5. Tree of life

A humongous and flourishing tree
With its roots spread far and wide
Numerous offshoots from it that it can't just hide
Society, people, family, friends, siblings
A fine meshwork of connections and relations twinkling
Innumerable people we connect and maybe just interact
They form the basis of our lives in fact
People from all walks , varied experiences
Maybe they share a few words or sentences
They groom us, build us, break us, protect us
Like tree branches , our lives get entwined
Leaves, flowers and fruits bloom and are designed
Life is a journey where you share, you learn
And love, respect along the way you earn
This is the true treasure you ought to conserve
Live life, love life
It has so much for you in reserve....

# 6. Life- A Roller Coaster Ride

Full of ups and downs
Smiles and frowns
Life throws lemons at you
Some moments it swells you up with gleam
It gives you many and then fulfils those dreams
Dreams that you start living for
The ones that slowly creep through your door
And then there are few of those moments that feel
shattering
You feel disconnected from life that was till now
tethering
Amidst this roller coaster ride of life, do remember one
thing dear
Don't forget to keep your loved ones near
Because in those disheartening and dark paths
Only they will be the ones who will seem like rays of
hope and comfort
Hold them, cherish them to sail through in those times of
purport

Life will surely show you many facets
It's only love and faith that will act like hatchet
To shatter those times of illusion
Rise , rise my love beyond the leaps and bounds of such
confusion....

# 7. Adolescence - Roses with thorns

After the innocence of childhood
Lays ahead ,a step before you enter adulthood
A stage of life called adolescence
A phase where nothing  makes sense
New physical, mental and emotional avenues lay ahead
All inhibitions, hesitations where you tend to shed
Life all of a sudden becomes all rosy and flowery
We shun all boundaries and shed all worry
People call you a rebel for no reason
All we are trying to do is being experimental with no
treason
There's a surge of energy, boundless, limitless
Just remember try not to make it a mess
Grow, explore, experiment, discover all you want ...my
love
Maybe its too early ,yet try to remember this norm
Life is a bed of roses but they always come with thorns...

# 8. University- What a life!!!

It's a whole new world that you step in
It seems a new life that preps you in
A plethora of knowledge and information
That we have to grasp in summation
Living in hostel... away from home
Having meals cooked in mess and not by Mom
That mixed feeling of freedom and anxiety
Life throws at you a garden of variety
Late night movies, reading in library.. what contrasts
This one is a life in our memories that forever lasts
A life that teaches us lessons for life
Sometimes sweet but at times sharp as a knife
This phase and place transforms ,breaks ,builds ,hones
Keep this life close to the heart ,treat it as a  milestone...

# 9. Step Into The Real World!

It's time to leave the flowery world behind
Although life has so far been very kind
But here lays ahead a world that awaits
Life will throw at you numerous challenges
Some simple to tide over and some with hinges
Time to be practical , to be as they say REAL
More of mind and less of heart and feel
De novo problems that we got to deal
In ways that we have never seen
Don't lose heart my love nor fade away your sheen
Don't forget to remember that this is just another phase
Howsoever we might feel that life has become a race
Even if it feels so, go ahead and conquer
Just do what's needed and don't ponder
And emerge as a winner on the other side of it
Because this is LIFE and this is how it will hit...

# 10. Soulmate Found!

That miraculous moment ..
Butterflies in your tummy
Life suddenly becomes a bed of roses
That one face that your heart chooses
That one voice which sounds so musical
You listen to it and go hysterical
Love is the name of this magical feeling
Makes you forget all wounds , it's so healing
If we are fortunate enough to find that ONE
Hold on to him for life and then look for none
Souls unite under the starts and sun
That exactly is the moment when your life transforms
Keep that soulmate closest to your heart... hold him tight
For that's the one with whom you would want to grow
old and lose your sight...

# 11. Marriage- Glorious Beginning

With Soulmate, a new journey embarks,
Time to take vows after those love sparks.
A path that feels dubious yet certain,
The one which you want to take yet refrain.
So many feelings that you feel inside,
The only feeling that stays on being with him is Pride.
That moment when you hold his hand it becomes clear,
That is the only sound that you can eternally hear.
You lovingly and fondly take those pious vows,
And make promises to him to be there in highs and lows.
This marks the beginning of a glorious chapter of life,
The one where he is your MAN and you are his WIFE....

# 12. Together we make a family!

Two souls after they unite,
An angel comes to their respite.
Those tiny hands and feet,
That timid being when you touch and feel makes your
heart skip a beat.
That very first time when you look into those eyes,
With infinite dreams , full of truths and no place for lies.
Undoubtedly role and responsibilities change,
Those feel like a mountain to conquer in a range.
Despite all that fear and apprehensions,
The world expands in infinite dimensions.
That little angel suddenly gives you the strength,
And you feel determined to work incessantly and go to
any length.
To bring smile to that cute adorable face,
Thus begins a family, a source of eternal happiness that
you never have to chase...

# 13. Living for family- Choice or Not

Now that the structure is defined,
Roles in family are aligned.
What comes next is you start living those,
Stand upto the life standards that you chose.
You might stumble upon the roadblocks on the way,
There would be times that will make you feel sway.
What underlies all those hurdles is love.
Love that you had started with,
Love that is truth and not a myth.
But the real question here is this,
What exactly is it that holds this delicate bond together,
Because if it's love then it might get heavy and not just light as a feather.
The boundaries and definitions might get blurred in this equation,
You might wonder sometimes if Life is all about this relation...

# 14. Life is all about Agreeing to Disagree

Two different people, two separate thoughts
Difficult to see what is right and what is not.
Ever wondered what is marriage?
Partnership, companionship in a carriage.
What starts with love and respect might face hurdles of
arguments,
We agree on most things but also might have some
disagreements.
It's not about love having vanished or respect no more,
What marriage is all about is wanting to be with each
other to the core.
Good, Bad, Happy, Sad- this journey will give you all,
Now it's upto you either to envision big or get bothered
by small.
The measure of this bond is simple and straightforward
Even a single moment of happiness shared together-
move forward.
For life is so short and will be over before you even
know,

Fill it up with nothing but love and let the seeds of
happiness grow.
Agree to disagree even when you don't,
For what really matters in life is this beautiful bond.

# 15. Companionship- Bed of roses or Shrub of Thorns

Companionship as I would prefer to label it than
Marriage,
For this bond acts less like a river and more like a
barrage.
It's a partnership of equality,
Being single with no duality.
Equality not as genders or tasks,
But of respect and asks.
Nothing is perfect , not even this
It's entirely upto us to turn it into a bliss.
Love each other with no boundaries,
Share late night movies as well as laundries.
For this companionship is all about picking out thorns
from roses,
Choosing each other always, when no one else choses.

# 16. Midlife Crisis!

They say it strikes at Forty,
But who set that rule anyway.
The relationship that had been so perfect till now,
Suddenly seems to be hitting a row.
Gestures, love, respect everything starts falling short,
So many complaints, resentments and what not.
Second thoughts on the aptness of even having started
one,
All these years, all efforts gone to drain and go for a run.
Explanations, Justifications , Lamentations,
Is that how we had started it at denomination?
Maybe it's just human to err on that aspect,
Maybe every couple falls short of the desired respect.
Even if that is the case, isn't it time to realise the root
cause?
Isn't it better to sort out the differences rather than live
with remorse?
The answer to this is very personal and individual,
Break this habit of complaining before you become
habitual.

For all this is nothing but what's called Midlife crisis,
Always stay happy, content within this eternal
relationship's premises.

# 17. Cycle of Life

What comes after Life for sure
What is it that is supremely pious and pure.
In going through the process of life
We tend to forget the constant presence of a knife.
A knife called DEATH that is the ultimate truth,
A truth that gets buried in the layers of life and stays
there put.
The parents who we always thought were agile,
Suddenly grow old and look fragile.
The strong hands that held us together,
Now become weak and won't get better.
Shades of grey and white appear on hair and face,
They alarm us that time is here to end this race.
And one day something jolts and they are gone,
Lost in the skies leaving us behind all alone.

# 18. Growing Old - Not so Gold!

Here comes the tract when age is getting better of me,
I am hearing less and it's becoming difficult to see.
Skin wrinkles, memory fades, judgement abates,
Day to day work becomes a task,
Tears roll down cheeks for things that never flooded the
gates.
Kids complain of generation gap that we fail to
understand,
They don't have time to give , it becomes a demand.
In these gloomy times, I have a knight in shining armour,
My companion, my soulmate, my darling partner.
Thank stars that we both are growing old together,
When world around me is falling apart, you are there to
matter.
Hold my hands and sail me through this ordeal,
Let's walk besides each other in mutual feel.
Life has been unimaginably forgiving and blessed,
We have been walking with each other on this path, my
hands in your hand..

# 19. Together - In Sickness and In Health

Do you remember what we said to each other as
marriage vows,
That we will be together in sickness and health , be there
in highs and lows.
Life has given us ample opportunities to prove that,
And I have been fortunate to have you as my
companion,
I have found a partner in you - One in a Million.
We have been our biggest strengths,
Have stood by each other and gone to any lengths.
The journey with you has been nothing less than a bliss,
I have achieved all with you and nothing feels amiss.
At this juncture where life is about to set,
It feels that there is left no debt and nothing to fret.
We have led an accomplished life together,
Life's hat looks so beautiful with it's every feather.

# 20. Till Death Do Us Apart...

The Ultimate truth and reality of Life is this,
Those innumerable moments that we spent with each
other and others that we did miss.
We laughed together , we cried on things,
We had so much in common yet our lives had different
meanings.
This journey has been together yet apart,
The end is here that makes me wonder where did we
start.
Life together maybe didn't go as we had imagined,
Yet we both gave our best and our lives synced.
No doubts about this that we had our differences,
At times it even felt that we had lost track of it's
nuances.
Suffocation, frustration, irritation was all a part,
But this is also a fact that we never could stay apart.
Our lives were complete with each other,
Seasons changed but the love never withered.
I will keep holding your hand , till the end from the start,
Only you will be my soulmate, till Death do us apart..

# 21. Life- What is it Anyways..

Existence - starts with a bare body,
Soaked in blood and flesh, looks so shoddy.
We step into this world, we do things,
We try to carve a niche, we work so hard to be
something.
Make and break relations, meet people and they also
depart,
One thing that stays constant is this life as it was since
the start.
After all these years of living it, it has revealed itself to
me,
Life isn't a form , a body, things or achievements as we
take it to be,
It's a never ending energy, a flow that is indestructible
,just let it be.
Embrace it with open hearts and arms, live it to the
fullest,
Breathe in it, Feel it, Grow in it, Rise and fall in it.
Just don't give up on it, just not yet,

Live Life to the fullest with whatever it gives and
whatever is left..